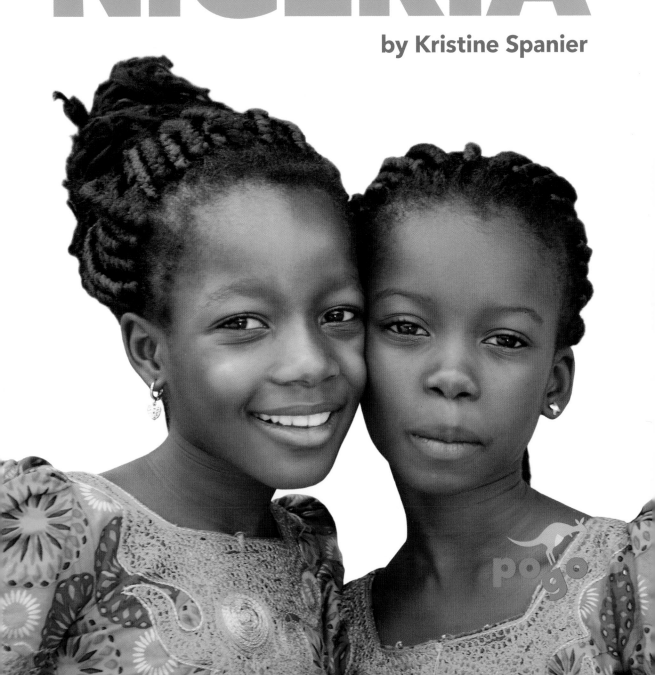

ALL AROUND THE WORLD
NIGERIA

by Kristine Spanier

Ideas for Parents and Teachers

Pogo Books let children practice reading informational text while introducing them to nonfiction features such as headings, labels, sidebars, maps, and diagrams, as well as a table of contents, glossary, and index.

Carefully leveled text with a strong photo match offers early fluent readers the support they need to succeed.

Before Reading

- "Walk" through the book and point out the various nonfiction features. Ask the student what purpose each feature serves.
- Look at the glossary together. Read and discuss the words.

Read the Book

- Have the child read the book independently.
- Invite him or her to list questions that arise from reading.

After Reading

- Discuss the child's questions. Talk about how he or she might find answers to those questions.
- Prompt the child to think more. Ask: Many different languages are spoken in Nigeria. What languages do you hear where you live?

Pogo Books are published by Jump!
5357 Penn Avenue South
Minneapolis, MN 55419
www.jumplibrary.com

Library of Congress Cataloging-in-Publication Data

Names: Spanier, Kristine, author.
Title: Nigeria / by Kristine Spanier.
Description: Minneapolis: Jump!, 2020.
Series: All around the world | "Pogo Books"
Includes bibliographical references and index.
Identifiers: LCCN 2018044386 (print)
LCCN 2018045136 (ebook)
ISBN 9781641286534 (ebook)
ISBN 9781641286503 (hardcover : alk. paper)
ISBN 9781641286510 (pbk.)
Subjects: LCSH: Nigeria—Juvenile literature.
Classification: LCC DT515.22 (ebook)
LCC DT515.22 .S64 2020 (print) | DDC 966.9—dc23
LC record available at https://lccn.loc.gov/2018044386

Editor: Susanne Bushman
Designer: Leah Sanders

Photo Credits: Lingbeek/iStock, cover, 8-9 (foreground); ariyo olasunkanmi/Shutterstock, 1; Pixfiction/Shutterstock, 3; Education Images/Getty, 4, 16-17; Fabian Plock/Alamy, 5; Hemis/Alamy, 6-7; s_oleg/Shutterstock, 8-9 (background); Friedrich Stark/Alamy, 10; peeterv/iStock, 11 (foreground); sumroeng chinnapan/Shutterstock, 11 (background); Jerry Chidi/iStock, 12-13; bonchan/Shutterstock, 14, 19; Kevin C. Cox/Getty, 15; JohnnyGreig/iStock, 18-19; Irene Becker/Getty, 20-21; Janusz Pienkowski/Shutterstock, 23.

Printed in the United States of America at Corporate Graphics in North Mankato, Minnesota.

TABLE OF CONTENTS

CHAPTER 1

WELCOME TO NIGERIA!

Would you like to see Zuma Rock? It is 2,379 feet (725 meters) high! Or spot baboons in a national park?

Zuma
Rock

Does crossing a swinging bridge above a forest **canopy** sound fun? Then you would love Nigeria. Welcome!

About 250 different **ethnic** groups live in Nigeria. Many have their own languages. The Hausa is the largest group. Another large group is the Yoruba. This group honors its past through music, art, and festivals.

WHAT DO YOU THINK?

English is the official language here. Yet not everyone can speak it. What challenges do you think this might create?

Hello!

The National **Mosque** is in Abuja. It was built in 1984. Abuja is the **capital**. The **president** is the head of the government. This leader is elected every four years. The National Assembly makes the laws.

National Mosque

TAKE A LOOK!

Nigeria's **coat of arms** has many **symbols**. What do they mean?

1 eagle: strength
2 horses: dignity
3 shield: fertile soil
4 white Y: Niger River and Benue River
5 red flowers: beauty of the nation
6 country **motto**

About half of the people live in **rural** areas. To get around, they ride donkeys or bikes. Some walk. In the desert, they may ride camels.

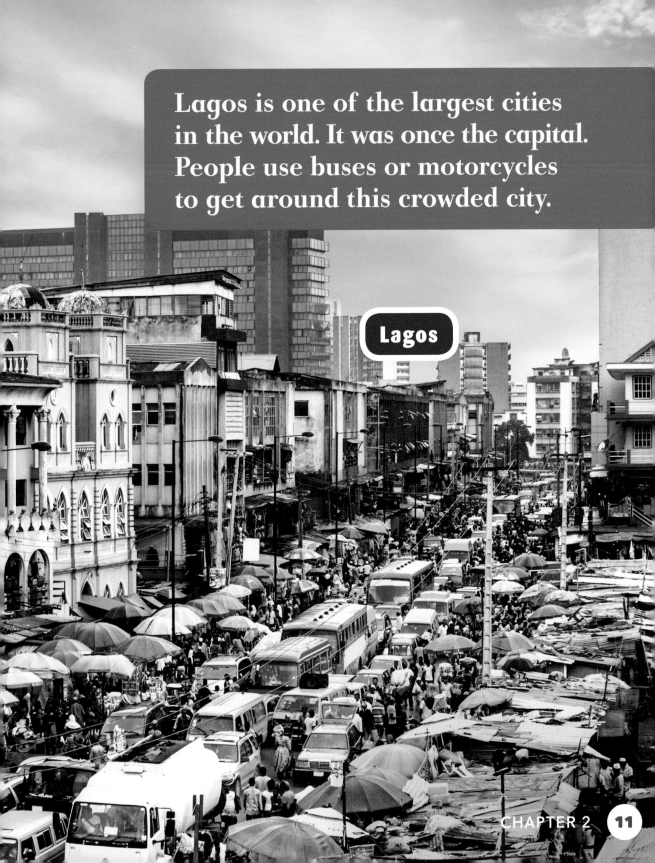

Lagos is one of the largest cities in the world. It was once the capital. People use buses or motorcycles to get around this crowded city.

Lagos

mangrove forest

Rolling **plains** are in the north. Mangrove forests grow where the Niger River meets the coast.

Yankari National Park is in the center. Swamps and grasslands are here. Spot baboons. What else? Giraffes. Elephants. Hyenas.

DID YOU KNOW?

In rural areas, high winds blow from December until March. This is known as the harmattan. A hazy red cloud forms from the dust.

CHAPTER 3

NIGERIA'S PEOPLE

Fufu makes a tasty meal. This is yam balls dipped in stew. People also like boiled plantains. They mix them with beans and palm oil.

fufu

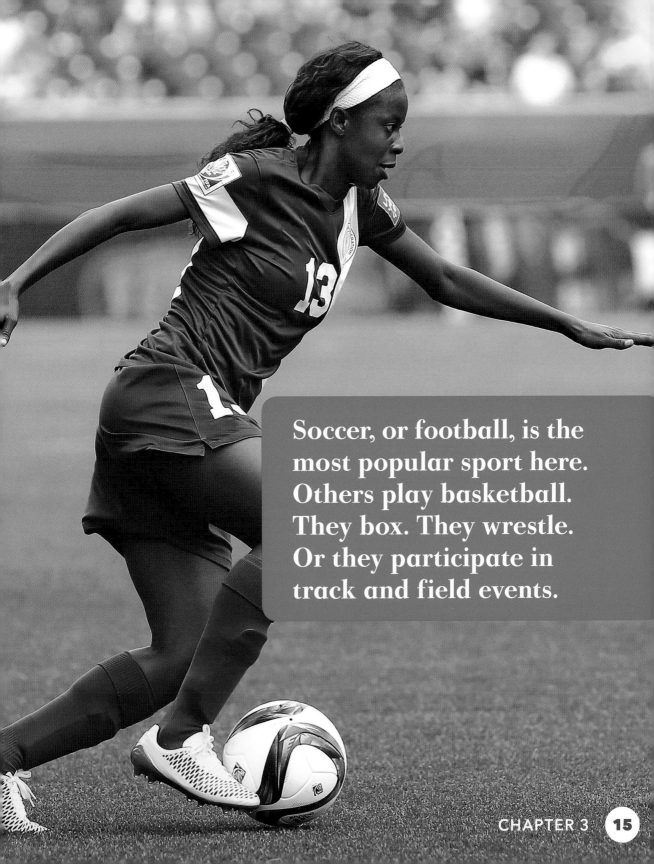

Soccer, or football, is the most popular sport here. Others play basketball. They box. They wrestle. Or they participate in track and field events.

Most children begin school when they are six years old. Primary school lasts for six years. Students wear uniforms. Many lessons are taught in English. Some students do not go on to secondary school. Instead, they help out at home. Or they begin working.

WHAT DO YOU THINK?

It is free to go to school here. But families must pay for books, supplies, uniforms, and building fees. Do you think families should pay for these items? Why or why not?

More than half of the workers here are farmers. What **crops** do they grow? Cocoa beans. Peanuts. Corn. Yams. Rice. Many farmers raise goats, sheep, and cattle.

Some people work in the oil industry. Petroleum products are important **exports**. Others work from home. They make pottery, jewelry, wood carvings, and woven mats and bags.

yams

A fishing festival called Fashin Ruwa is in Argungu each year. Men fish using nets and baskets. They compete to catch the biggest fish. The New Yam Festival celebrates the yam **harvest**. People sing. They dance. And they eat yams!

Nigeria is an interesting country. What would you want to see here first?

DID YOU KNOW?

Nigeria was a British colony until 1960. Independence Day is celebrated on October 1.

Fashin Ruwa

QUICK FACTS & TOOLS

NIGERIA

Location: western Africa

Size: 356,669 square miles (923,768 square kilometers)

Population: 203,452,505 (July 2018 estimate)

Capital: Abuja

Type of Government: federal presidential republic

Languages: English and more than 500 traditional languages

Exports: petroleum, cocoa, rubber

Currency: naira

canopy: The upper level of a rain forest, consisting mostly of branches, vines, and leaves.

capital: A city where government leaders meet.

coat of arms: A design on a shield that identifies a noble family, person, city, or organization.

crops: Plants grown for food.

ethnic: Of or having to do with a group of people sharing the same national origins, language, or culture.

exports: Products sold to different countries.

harvest: The gathering of crops that are ready to eat.

mosque: A building where Muslims worship.

motto: A short phrase that states a belief.

plains: Large, flat areas of land.

president: The leader of a country.

rural: Related to the country and country life.

symbols: Letters, characters, or signs used instead of a word or group of words.

Nigeria's currency

INDEX

TO LEARN MORE

Finding more information is as easy as 1, 2, 3.

1 Go to www.factsurfer.com

2 Enter "Nigeria" into the search box.

3 Click the "Surf" button to see a list of websites.

FACT SURFER